Strings of Shining Silence
Earth-Love Poems

Strings of Shining Silence
Earth-Love Poems

by
Raphael Block

Poetic Matrix Press

Poetic Matrix Press
John Peterson, Publisher
www.poeticmatrix.com

May these droplets water your heart,
for the earth thirsts for your love.

Dear Peter,

I hope you'll enjoy many of these pieces.

With all good wishes,

Raphael

Preface

It's a joy to share with you the experiences in these poems. With the benefit of hindsight, I see that my central concern throughout the collection is our relationship to this wondrous earth.

Our very human world is also present with its play of light and shadow, and love's compass, spanning the unlikely and unthinkable.

For the past seven years, a life-threatening disease, Crohn's, has played a major role in intensifying my appreciation and gratitude for the moments of each day. These feelings are, hopefully, reflected in the poems.

May these verses be a source of surprise, discovery, and uplift for you. Please feel free to share them, within the courtesies of copyright, in whatever way comes most naturally to you, be it song, dance, drawing, reciting, posting, and more.

Acknowledgments

I feel both happy and grateful that John Maas chose to compose four of these poems into songs for choirs. The first page of his scores is included in the final section of this book. John is very open to them being performed. You can listen to them in electronic format at his website http://johnmaas.webs.com and also access the full score.

I would like to thank *Sufi Journal* for the magnificent job they do of combining poetry and photography. In particular, for publishing "New Leaf" from this book (*Sufi* Issue 85) and "Honey" in *Songs from a Small Universe* (*Sufi* Issue 86). I'm also grateful to Larry Robinson, former mayor of Sebastopol, potter, poet and ardent exponent of the oral tradition, for sending out some of these poems on his E-Poem a Day.

Many of these poems have been much improved by feedback from my fellow poets in our critique group *Wellspring.* My deepest thanks to Terry Ehret, former Sonoma County Poet Laureate, co-founder of *Sixteen Rivers Press,* author of four poetry books, and beloved teacher, whose editorial suggestions always prove invaluable. Also, thanks to Carolyn Miller for her meticulous copyediting and many useful suggestions and to Nan Hopkin for her guidance. I have left out much punctuation to help pieces flow more easily. All errors are my own.

This book could not have been born without my publisher, John Peterson, with his far-reaching vision of poetry's role in our society, and his very practical support.

I would also like to express my delight with Judyth Greenburgh's cover design.

Contents

Strings of Shining Silence

Lost Riches

Opening to a Dance

Bird Suite

What Will Remain

Composition For Choir by John Maas
and Songs by Raphael Block

About the Author

Strings of Shining Silence
Earth-Love Poems

Strings of Shining Silence

To Her Loveliness

each crinkly leaf
each trailing yellow shamrock
or clover crown

each floating spore
swallow swoop
canopy of thousands dancing to the wind

each set of see-through humming wings
open-throated quaver
bright-spiked shoot

each fledgling oak
tottering on
its slender stem

each scarlet neckband
draped 'round
golden poppy

each pair of gold-rimmed coupling beetles
sunbathing mottled rock
swan-winged scented iris

binds us to her loveliness.

Blue Moon

The moon came to sip
    dew at my table, and liking it,
        stayed awhile.

Soon she slipped into a nearby
    puddle to dip and bathe,
        bending the trees
            with her glory.

The cat, desperate
    to join this lunar party,
        caterwauled like crazy
            until I padded up
                to grant his wish.

He sprinted toward
    her silvery sheen,
        only to find
            she had whisked
                back into the sky

leaving us both behind
    yowling and baying.

Bearded Iris

Searing brown-and-white-striped
　　zebras gallop across petal plains
intercepted by a golden mane—
　　ah! the scent!
One small black beetle
　　foraging in pollen heaven
rolls onto rich purple veins.

Dewdrops cling
　　to a threesome
of dorsal wings
　　sheltering a whorl of whelps.

Tightly wrapped buds
　　twinned to long green stems
crouch and leap in pride
　　from pointed leaves, their den
laired in muck's mysteries.

Violet-drenched tracks trail away
　　into cupped translucent skins.

Queen Anne's Lace

Summer nebulae open all
　　over the meadows
　　　　and roadsides.
White star clusters fade
　　in waves folding
　　　　into soft-sided cups
filled with a bounty
　　of beetle-like seeds.

Bunched ribs and hoops
　　unfurl by slow degrees
　　　　into open arms
their legacy ready,
　　like mine, to leap
　　　　out of its nest
fly with a gust
　　cling to any passerby.

Dripping Grace

My ears fill with
   dripping, dancing
drops, although it's
   June in California.

The light gray sky
   without a break
drapes over redwood
   peaks and oaks.

A whisper of leaves
   among red-leafed plum,
catkin strands, wild
   swaying oats, rain-soaked
darkened deer.

Come to the Shore

Mighty ebb and surge
   flings flatfish
with jutting ribs
   among kelp bouquets
sprawling on the sands

bound by fine green strands
   to marbled godwits piping
ancient songs in a round
   of spindly legs and juddering beaks
jabbing at a feast

wild waves roar
   charge up secret passageways
cascading into creatured pools
   and spiraling withdraw

drizzling mist releases
   swirling tabla rhythms
ta tiki-ta, ta tiki-ta,
   tiki ta-ta, tiki ta-ta

cones tilt
   like crows at rest
sway in moist dune pines
   while updrafts
sweeten and purge

until my mind's return
   urges me to swoop
and hunt for that
   which can't be tracked

Autumn Hollows

Flash of white-tailed
   deer, scudding hooves.
     I veer down a track
past a clean-picked
   skeleton, furred torso
    almost intact

its hollow-ribbed cavity
   filling with a drift
    of acorns
      and oak leaves.

Again we meet—
   three does and I
       freeze—holding
each other
   with softly
    melting eyes.

Song Original

A dream remembered on reading Denise Levertov's "A Tree Telling of Orpheus."

Waking from thick-wooded slumber
    notes begin to surge within my sap.
        They swarm through my veins
        vibrating with the eddying air,
my roots stir to the strain of chords
    dying to dance.

My branches sway while
    from my crown issue sounds,
    the pulse of unfurling leaves
        high-pitched melodies
        that know my name
    that know each atom of my being
so sweet and wounding.

    All night I revel
abandoned to its might
even as my trunk
    harbors a secret fear.

    All through that day I marvel—
yet before three full moons
steal over my limbs
    mists dim my remembrance.

Weighted by pelting rains,
    countless weathered seasons
one star-filled sky
    a slivered moon
    slides down a beam
        splintering my being.

My screams tear at the air
              until notes
long-driven deep within
              gush out—
              rippling in pools
In all you are and do
my ancient song sings you.

Waylaid

Startled, the stag
  and his does bolt
    under silhouetted firs
    and across louring
  clouds hunched
on the horizon.

Meowing, a cat
  rubs against my legs.
    As I bend low
      to stroke her
        the last birdsong
      gives way to a tidal
    cricket orchestra,
  a star spills out
from a crack of sky.

I trudge uphill, engulfed
  by bristling worries
    until the rising
    sonorous tide
  snaps me
back once more.

Clouds vanish,
  stars skip
    out to dance—
    a firefly plane
  noses its way
into the silence.

Lizard

Sweep of tail
   bulge of red-brown body
webbed feet planted firmly
   eyes warily watching all degrees
how zippily you dart
   into a rustle of leaves.

Come again, come again
   to bathe in the sun with me!

The Violinist

*Inspired by fiddle player, Martin Hayes,
and violinist, Dmitri Berlinsky.*

ringlets jiggle
   mustang manes
    field-ripple
fiddle rears

whistling owls trace
   inky skies
    wood elves prance
leap fingerboard

long-held voices vault
   out of vast rounded vessel
    sail haunting pipes
mouth harp snatches

earth's deep sorrow-well
   swells into its ancient
    gut warm pith
her bow skip-bounces

over string slides
   torso reels
    feet rock-planted
newborn cries

Strings of Shining Silence

When shadows lengthen,
our breaths grow closer, and
bundled bodies huddle against
drizzle-slanting snow and rain.

To warmth we turn,
the nearness of a cello heartbeat;
strings of shining silence
fill my chest with crimson tones.

Each in-breath spins me into soundness
while with each outward rush of air—
though winds may shriek and squall,
clouds flash and crack—

shafts of sunlight— somehow—
slip through my being and unfold.

Doesn't Everything Sing When We Have Ears?

If you seek subtlety,
watch the seahorse-tips
of a fern uncurl.

If you want magic,
gaze at a full-blown
dandelion head and
puff! like the child
you are and were.

If you need complexity,
find hazel leaves
and contrast and compare.

If you treasure praise,
why, there are coral
bells a-pealing by
the road's edge.

If majesty is your heart's
desire, look up
the jeweled bark
of a Douglas fir.

If you seek humility,
the large-leafed dock
rescuer for stings and wounds
sits quietly there.

If you need adventure,
venture into poison oak
trails and mark
your way without fear.

If you crave ecstasy,
let full-throated warblers
ring throughout
your orchard.

Wild white stars
of cucumber vines
are waving to enter
your open-gated garden.

Lost Riches

The London Tinker

His clanging bell rouses
the neighborhood
while his hoarse bellows
drown the clip-clopping
of his companion

> *Any ol' i'on*
> *scrap for sale*
> *   any ol' i'on*
> *scrap for sale…*

Following in his wake
black, leaden, whispered tales
of stripped roofs, gutter pipes—
empty houses laid bare

We never knew when
his cacophonous cry
would next be heard

Now, heaters, blenders,
broken down toasters,
spill into the street
          Nobody to pick up—
no one to collect—
   dump
            landfill
overwhelmed

Rusting car carcasses
pile in ditches——

      Any ol' i'on
scrap for sale
        any ol' i'on
scrap for sale…

      his echoing cry
and horse's hooves
no longer heard

Lost Faith

דע לפני מי אתה עומד
Know whom you stand before

When we went to Temple on Sabbath and Holy
Days, inscribed in gold letters above the ark shone those
Hebrew words, while the men, including—
unforgivably— my father, discussed business, the
weather, and the likely soccer result of the home team
that day.

The sacred text hummed by the cantor was all but
drowned out by their animated conversations that
paused occasionally for the *Amidah,* the "Standing Prayer"
recited three times daily, "Lord, open my lips and my
mouth will sing your praises…" and the *Mourner's
Kaddish,* with its magnetic, somber tones and climactic,
"Blessed, praised, glorified, exalted, extolled, mighty,
upraised, and lauded be the Name of the Holy One.
Blessed is He beyond any blessing and song, praise and
consolation that are uttered in the world…"

Bombarded by the steady rumble of the men around
me, my piety crumbled.

For fourteen years, the time Jacob labored to win his
true love, after cheating his twin of his birthright, I held
fast to my indignation, until scales began to slip away
and I found myself, like a fish, embraced by water— the
vibrant waters of that unnameable presence.

Clay Spirit

Breakfasting
    I feel the warm clay bowl
        of my mother's making
            cradling my fingers.

Solidly thrown
    her name etched on the bottom
        the beige glaze
            reflects a range

of creamy whites to speckled browns
    just like her eyes.
        My hands rest
            on its generous rim.

What feelings traveled through her hands
    to mine? She who transmitted so much
        so much that I rejected
            and now hold sacred.

Rattlesnake Grass

You must have seen the dewy grasses dressed in Juning gold,
each twin top streaked with reddish-purple capes,
each lush, layered body tanned in tawny shades.
And beside them, soft ears of venetian rose, hair-like strands
perched on willowy stems.

A touch of swaying bells, faint rattling shakes,
and you find the youthful wonder
that sent you halfway around the world
quite near, quite near.

New Leaf

I am silent.
  You are a leaf.
  Your edges enfold me,
my jade veins come to life.

I uncurl
  into your embrace.
  Our lips meet,
honey flows.

On Dropping a Jar of Honey

Faster than gravity
  it slipped, then shattered
    on the stone floor,
the jar my friend just
  brought all the way
    from Rochester.

Her nose wrinkled,
  eyes widened, brow lines
    wriggled. My jaw dropped,
I swallowed hard, stared
  at the ground, willing
    a crater to appear.

When the real
  bombshell falls—
    my love's passing
shock waves sweep
  my smithereened body
    along the moon's shores

until hunger finally
  drives me to a cellar
    where I discover stacks
and stacks of your
  honey-filled jars
    waiting on the shelves.

Riches in the Night

In the middle of the night, they banged on my door.
It opened in the middle of that night

to two well-built strangers.
The taller, silver hair swept back, quietly spoke

You have an almost priceless cooking set
that we have come to collect—

to return to its rightful owner.
In answer to my dazed looks

he crossed the room in a couple of strides
and pulled out from under my bed

three ceramic tureens.
My mouth gaped, eyes burned

at the ancient glazes drawn like veils.
In the middle of that night, the taller said

We will send them to the East
where they will fetch a good price.

You may keep the smallest for soups.
His companion showed me a small mark

in the sole of his shoe
then pointed towards my foot

and in the middle of that night
made the same impression in my sole.

This will serve as the key. So saying
they left, but by what means I do not know.

Once

After John Donne (1572-1631)

Once, your arched feet and limbs stretched
to tease the ground, your gesturing
arms sang to the sky, the swish of your black skirt
overturned my heart. But now, they've wound
themselves into a stranglehold around
this tightened chest.   Expel my breath!
Plow these barren furrows! Seven Sisters light
all my belly's sorrows. When will Orion
sheathe his sharp sword that stabs so darkly
in the night? Will the ocean waves bear my despair
on their ceaseless slap and roll?
Ah! But this salted grief
has sweetened— the tears I pour
taste more and more like seasoned wine.

My Love Beyond

My love lives so far away
                              so far away
yet we share

                              bare hearts
along bared wires

                              our whispered words
balance perilously

                              as starling silhouettes
on wind-stripped lines

                              "couldn't you just travel
there?"

                              I might, I might
but a jealous lover

                              cracked open our
inner chambers

                              dispelling all dramas
and reactions

                              changing our chemistry
and composition

                              into one lone cry

How Can I Explain?

How can I explain
       that I still miss

the curves of your loving arms
       where we whispered
tender words

your breasts that nurtured
       our bonnie one
for years

       the hidden crevasses
that opened with
       intimate glances
our ignited passions

       the endless lapping gulf
swaying under the moon's
       dark tides

fluctuating phases
       of silence, laughter
anger, pain
       gushing, swelling, waning

your so eloquent
       twist of lip
flashing eye
       raised crescent brow.

Although the mounds
       of your fertile earth
dissolved ages ago—
       how can I explain?

Drink My Blood, Lord

After John Donne's Holy Sonnets (1609-1610)

Drink my blood, Lord—
turn it into the crimson red
of a winter sunset.

Cicadas sing to their beloveds
from timpani guts, while
strips of cerulean
dangle between darkening
clouds. Deer hunger
to feast on moonlit cereal
grasses, and I wait here
thirsting for you.

How long can moths hover
and flutter, bats beat
sonic airways before
the two collide?

So, drink my blood, Lord—
let it seep swiftly
into that deep violet sky
until night begins to shine.

Burning Questions

Listen to the burning
    questions
that sear, singe
    scald and scold.

Are they
    a fiery or somber dance
begging for my feet
    to stomp the floor?

A song
    curled tightly
        in my throat
wailing a few tentative notes
    or a full-bellied roar?

A glowing palette
    of yarn beckoning for
        a patterned home?

Or a fallen trunk
    calling for mallet
        chisel, sharp
            smoldering eye?

A rock yearning
    to be struck
        and shaped?

A hand
    readying to strum
in rhythm
    to my pounding
        heart?

I Become

And I become a child again
among the grasses
of towering oats and rye,
Shasta daisies overhead,
sharp lavender within
fingers' reach
a forest of lush leaves

as a bumblebee whirls
into tumbling pollen
cupful after cupful,
reels into a spider's
web, sheer weight
until it frees itself
to go on foraging.

Sheened ladybugs scuttle
up and down stems
on six wheeling spindles,
shiny beetles sprawl
on broad green plains,
a tiny spider
huddles while

an orange-tipped
spider moth stalks.
Beyond the buzzing,
the air thickens
with beaks
and twitters.

Won't we all meet
sometime, somewhere?
Will I tumble gladly
into your arms,
belly, jaws, skin,
And what then?

First and Last

My words spill out
    like sharp rocks
        the first time we meet—
            I stumble and bleed

We climb meadow slopes,
    uncover love
        in bloom
            make daisy chains

Years later, in that one call—
    we pick up the gray mountain
        shot with blue
            of our panic and distress

Now shadows beseech
    a crescent moon.
        Your laughter's waned
            and I must carry on

Wild Grasses

This hermit watches
    sheets of mist
        sweep

across the yard
    hears the rain
        drip.

He listens inside—
    the hurt of feeling
        alone

has ripened
    to embrace
        large-eyed does

who come closer—
    chew juicy
        wild oats.

He dreams of scything
    the overlong
        bowed grasses.

And when
    it's his call
        wishes to go

as graciously
    as their seeds
        borne on the wind.

Where I Dwell

Yellow monkey flowers
    and purple beard tongues
      spring between dark red
          rocks in an ancient wall.

My limbs reach through
    those vast grained surfaces
      only to return again.

Nests perch, now full, now emptied
    of fledgling dreams flitting out
      on flashing wings.

And once the chirping ceases
    my heart takes off
      following the swift's path.

The wind's reflection pales, sunlight
    spikes surprise— a sweep
      of love and all words wilt
         before my crumbling mind.

Architect

Clambering around her main frame
she lays cross-beams
across each arterial ray.

They come out of her core
as she slithers
first one way
then another,
checking all crossing-points.

Such silky light—
her structure reflects
the sun!

She freezes at a sudden tug,
curls up like one
of her catches, then
dives to the center.

Her temple swings
elegantly in the breeze,
two long guy ropes
anchored to a fence,
two to the rose that fills
her net with aphids.

Her legs sweep side
to side, torso tilts
as she dances
in tighter rings
feet nimbly feeling each tie,
each strut in place.

I hear the click of spinnerets
as my lifelines, too,
are set.

Blazing Trees

You have only to see
the blazing sunset through
the trees to be
in that dazzling presence
and catch a voice saying
"Take off your masks!"

With a clatter they land
all around, but you barely
notice because the fire
in your heart is bursting
toward that bright glow
on the horizon.

And when its last
glimmering rays are gone—
from human sight—
you're left with a gateway
that will open
even in your dark hour.

Opening to a Dance

Harp

My
palm b-
rushes agai-
nst last year's lily
of-the-Nile. Its stems
vibrate like a muted
harp to which gol-
dfinches in a nea-
rby bush sin-
g and ju-
mp.

Teen Outline

Suddenly, the outline
   of my daughter on the phone
once clear and distinct
   seems blurred and out of sync.

She stands there before me
   lips pattering, body jiggling
voice skydiving
   as I rub my eyes in disbelief.

"Dad, come and see!"
   has set like a sun
and this awesome being
   now won't be pigeonholed

as she cheerily waves goodbye—
   blowing a kiss
starts the engine
   of my heart sputtering

and revving, drives off
   into her own life.

Opening To A Dance

Pulled between a lull after lunch
   or plunging to the next task
      I make myself wait.
Did my ancestors not sing thanks
   in the shade of noon?
      I inwardly begin to chant

Ey-na, ey-na-heh,
  ey-na, ey-na heh,
ey-na, ey-na-heh,
  ey-na, ey-na-heh…

Curled leaves fly
  into my lap, while
    silhouetted on the ground
a dance is going down
  shimmering, whirling,
    flourishing, swirling

Ey-na, ey-na-heh,
  ey-na, ey-na heh,
ey-na, ey-na-heh,
  ey-na, ey-na-heh…

Chiseled faces surface,
  dark-skinned, brown
    eyes twinkling
shadowed feet rising
  and turning in
    shafts of light

Ey-na, ey-na-heh,
  ey-na, ey-na heh,
ey-na, ey-na-heh,
  ey-na, ey-na-heh…

Twin Sheep

My new neighbor
   was wheeled in at 3 a.m.
      babbling and unwell

He turned the TV on loud—
   I fumed and cursed.
      A nurse gave me ear plugs

And how we snored!
   Like two grizzled old sheep
      bedded in a pen

Small Comforts

At the end of the ward's long corridor
    the radiator knobs glow
amethyst as I struggle toward them
    with my catheter stand.

Their warmth pulls me along
    to where a pine's
spiraling needles splash against
    the large window.

Somewhere I know the knobs
    are plain chrome
but I prefer to bear this precious image
    that draws me slowly there.

Inbox

oh Lord, let me not be
  just a window
    in your daily schedule
as so often you are
  in mine

rather, I beg,
  let me occasionally,
    at least,
be an empty inbox
  for your messages

however inconvenient
  following them
    may prove to be

Grounded

my cat catches up,
   makes a sound, rolls
     onto his side on
   the dark ground,
motioning to be stroked

sprawling and turning,
   he draws me down
   from the plots and plans
fiercely droning inside

back to the soles
   of my feet. His ears
   prick, body follows
like a tuft of snaking fur

leaving me free
   to wade through waves
   of crickets and
scented evening air

while a half-moon arches
   her back to Venus—
     both close enough to touch—
   casting light among
the shadow clusters.

At Wild Flour

There is a bakery nearby
   where, drawn by warm
aromas, people enter
   to watch the bread makers
up to their elbows in dough.

Now and then, one opens
   the oven and fishes for
steaming loaves with a long paddle
   to load the waiting trays.

What if time were such
   a loaf, and each slice
tasted both sweet
   and sour, tinged
like a sunset

with apricot orange and
   cranberry red, dotted with
poppy seed clouds
   and cardamom sprinkles?

Each bite oozes
   rosemary, thyme—
every mouthful
   secretes smooth
and grainy textures.

And what if I were to treat time
   as elastic as dough—each
moment, each hour,
   stretching, leavening
like their humblest bread!

Reflection

Sounds of hooting laughter
   leap up the path
high-pitched yelps
   issue from my daughter's mouth
as he chases her
   toward the house.

Chatter and banter
   fill the kitchen
overflow the rooms
   while they cook, tease, and joke
following the recipe steps:

   1. Mince onion— "How?"
     "What size do they mean?"
   2. Dry spinach— "With what?"

Resting in an easy chair
   I catch sight
reflected in my window
   a tender kiss.

Poetry Can't

Poetry can't catch the bullet
   leaving the gun—
though she might.
   She takes me on flights,
lands on scorched runways
   shudders and shakes up
all my beliefs.

Poetry won't stop me
   stumbling in the dark—
though she may.
   She'll croon in the night
to my twin
   longing and grief.

Poetry may not sate
   the starving—
though she might.
   She wakes me
to my own hunger
   leavens the bread
kindles irresistible scents.

She unleashes
   a pent-up panther,
shows me a way out
   of clawing despair,
leads me through
   her music to dance.

Within Easy Reach

Phosphorescent yellow
  far side in shadow
    golden apples hanging ready
on the three-pronged tree
  clustered like grapes
    under its rusty canopy

And what of my own life's fruit?

This is the season still
  for harvesting those years
    of tears, frosts of anger
shines of laughter
  that tempered and ripened
    each golden delicious

now at last within easy reach.

Rippling and Astir

There's a rippling
   in the air
      stealing

across the hillside
   misty sheets
      slant and race

toward
   this terrible
      thirst.

All green things
   are dressed in
      see-through pearls.

Droplets pounce, bounce
   polka dance on
      wooden posts.

Brushing, rushing
   shimmering
      bush and tree

limbs flap, sway
   opening to
      volleys' intensity.

A hushed soaring
   roars.

Bird Suite

What My Two Eyes See

A film of early protozoic life—
  brown blobs and tails swirl
in a clouded ring.
  Up they slowly rise
and fall again,
  circumscribed by the boundaries
of my aging eyes.
  But how the birds now sing!

Evening Swell

Hazelnuts are plumping
  their magenta-hued husks
    crowned by a crest. See
the squirrels secrete
  them long before
    they're ripe for you and me

Raindrops and robins alight
  trigger a trickle
    in the roadside creek, while
fresh green pine tips
  lean over a ditch of dock
    dandelion, wild peppermint

All hangs on the swell
  of trills and song in
    these burgeoning woods

Songster

Oh sweet loquacious songster
  I am your eager ear
    riding your streams and trills—

be my companion
  so once your notes have risen
    beyond range

into silence broken
  only by a breeze
    weighing on the leaves

I will not forget
  my pledge made
    during your ecstatic bursts

Sing to me, sing!
  so my heart may turn
    in twilight's ebb

and through the night
  be drawn
    along liquid ways

until your dawn song
  breaks its banks again

Little Bird

Is anything more precious
than the little caged bird
in our heart, desperately flapping
its wings against our cold bars—
dying to dip and dive,
even to hover in mid-air—
before singing its song
trilling its notes
knowing all creation's
molecules hear.

What is more dear than
this little held bird?

They Rise

They rise and melt,
  their great wings
    glinting in the sun
      as they sense the airways
        and follow, now
          this way, now that.

        They aren't flying
      in line, but more
      like a flowing
    seaward
  dissolving into
purple cloud.

To Sight

Oh glory be to sight
for the play of sun on hazy
trees, April yellow-greens,
shadows laze in still striped
bands as sparrows and woodland
birds edge morning on, traffic
roars soak into quiet hills.

Flowering periwinkle
tumbles down the banks
into morning-moistened grass.
The chorus builds, and I
am happy to be part of it
though one eye fails.

Thanksgiving

The little ones
    skip
        from twig
            to tree
                to tree
                    to twig
                        invisibly fast.

Overhead a large one soars.

Beneath black
    and white
        feathered stripes
            a dash of yellow
                flashes.

Among wilting flowers
    legumes and fruits
        the little ones
            busily twitter
                skirt and scoot
                    about this season
                    of seeds

signaling Thanksgiving.

Breath
    of eucalyptus
        inhales
            while blue jay
                hoarsely proclaims—
                It's always
                    thanksgiving.

What Will Remain

What Will Remain

Everything will be snatched
out of our limbs
as the fall winds
breeze, tease,
tug and swell,
remorselessly tearing
our leaves
of money, shredding
our looks and bodily sheaths.

What's left in the land?
Only the roots and ripples
of our laughter,
troughs of tears,
the draughts of love
that we bring.

So now it is fall,
leaves fly, fly
to the earth,
and when our need
is to cling,
aren't we held in embrace
by pattering rain?

For in the fragile
ribbed web of our being,
all is dissolving—
only the core remains.

Frida Kahlo's *Self-Portrait with Monkeys*

Their dark eyes are filled with questioning innocence. Hers are weary and aching. Their small hands grip her blouse, an arm clasps her neck, as if they, too, understand the weight of great sadness. Half-hidden by lily leaves, they squat and stand with momentary restraint.

Her body knows that the bird of paradise will wilt, die, and come again—that her white-breasted monkey friends will burst into cacophonous chatter, and vanish through the shaking, screeching tree-tops as suddenly as they appeared. This fragrant flame is her one hope.

So she carefully braids and ties her thick, black hair above her ashen face, propels herself to the easel, toward the blank canvas that has waited through the long, tremulous night for a blood infusion from her molten depths.

This Pain of Parting

You jump on
everything I say.
The air runs
rancid.
We wish for one more
pleasant time
but it's lost
among the rocks.

Stranded
whale
lashing tail
your pleading
eyes—this pain
of parting.

Toward last summer's
end
jet black
forces erupted
from your being
scalding
our skin.

Wounded
whales
tails lashing
eyes pleading—
this pain
of parting.

Now we've just spent
three weeks

basking in each
other's presence.
I lack
all elegance and clap
my demons on
to hasten
the moment.

Stranded
whale
lashed tail
pleading eyes—
this pain of parting.

Narcissus

I will get me to the bottom of the hill
    heaviness clawing at my belly
to smell the narcissus rows
    a dull whiff
I may see the first wild-berry flowers,
    smoldering
a red-tail perched on power lines
    shackled wings
spying out prey
    wild glowering
white plum blossom spills
    spewing fumes
scents onto the road
    suffocating those I love

I'll dally under the canopy of fresh green oak
    wallow in the mud
listening to the murmur of amber leaves
    savor simmering moans of my ghosts
I'll chat with each neighbor I meet
    every neighbor I'll greet
about this and that
    with a chameleon's mask
arriving home
    return in a funk
view the ebbing colors of our sun
    my color drains
while the cooing dove and children's cries
    into a cauldron of boiling darkness
fill the early evening air

I'll gaze with fresh eyes
    a pained stare

at the delicate lines on the calla lily's face
furrows my brow
seeing her spiraling sisters unfurl
catching myself so snagged
I'll hitch my hands to two trash cans
drag my well-tended load
towing them back along the pebble drive
the yoke and the goad
and stretch my neck to watch
crane to catch
the pygmy nuthatch tunneling for grubs
a glimpse of anything else
When I reach those narcissus,
yes, anything else
kneeling, I will bury my nose and rise with heaven's touch
but my own fallen, terrifying beauty

Day's End

Fetching the empty garbage cans,
I watch the entire sky turn into
a pair of thick indigo wings
crowned by the tufts of
a great horned owl,
her barred belly
brooding over
the day's end
hatches moonlit
dreams
of all
I
ditch
and
dump.

Who Speaks to the Trees?

Three massacres have I witnessed. Our one-legged
cousins lie sprawled on our Mother's dusty face.

> Yet I hear you
> I hear you
> I hear you
> weeping, bleeding, uprooted.

For one hundred years you faithfully gave your
quenching fruit, shelter and shade to all who came.
   Commit genocide? Not the bulldozer driver—his
kids need clothing and feeding. Nor the *compadres*
hammering stakes and setting irrigation for the new
cash crop— they have families and obligations. Nor the
owners, who believe a coastal touch of fog, perfect for
these grapes, will soon play upon our lips.
   And so, dear Mother, what can I say to you?
   How can I make amends?

*The "one-legged nation" are the trees and their spirits
   (Native American knowledge).*

Necklaces

You scatter your finest necklaces
  across the sky, dewdrops deftly hung
    on spider strands—
      pearls dazzling patches of night.

Thousands of crickets chorus up
  to the lights, bathing the listener
    in a thickness of sound as
      refreshing as the season's first swim.

How long, how long, have I
  been lulled and cosseted by
    the world wide web, paying
      only lip service to your gems?

In My Blood

running rivulets
  gushing wild—
swollen, bubbling streams
  water whorls patterned
like much-mended
  fishermen's nets
fingerprint swirls

can we, too,
  be the rain
falling down
  from dark clouds
knowing not
  where or how
we'll land?

A Rock by Walker Creek

Small white flowers flourish on your face, sheltered by your monumental arms. A vine clambers along your crevasses. On your leeward side, stained ocher, orange, white, and green create a sandstone sculpture blending with the 'scape.

White clouds twist and unfurl past a pale crescent moon. Ever unwinding coastal curls hover above a lone, dark silhouette skimming the greened oak and coyote bush clad hills.

A confluence of silences. Leaves-of-three bud in the breeze. Rifts and splits birth your offspring scattered on the slopes. Golden poppies and rosemary adorn your soft, grass hair.

On This January Day

under clear sky
  rhythmic movement
    swells the sea

woven beds
  of kelp
    bob and sway

an ozone-laden breeze
  sails over the green
    and rusty ice-plants

perched on sandstone
  while gull shadows
    clip the cliff-tops

cascades and cataracts
  meet and over-wash
    mussel-covered rocks

cormorants on
  ledges eye
    the tidal splash

churning waters
  scoop and crash
    in the fierce

heave of this
  perpetual
    outpouring

Naked Oak

My gnarled stumps
  expose vast sky
    one limb points cloudward—
  a frozen lightning fork.

Across my body spreads green and
  gray-white lichen, old man's beard dangles
    on my few branches, my underside
  teems with fungal tribes,
loosened bark, softness crumbles.

Wind whips willow sprigs,
  swarming blackberry vines,
    purple leaves of poison oak, scented
  honeysuckle twines, brown stems
of becoming-pink flowers.

All bound in spring's bright tunic
  while I bend closer, closer
    to the ground
  readying to receive me
unadorned, open-armed.

The Brook's Song to Spring

I stumble and slip-slide, spout and leap,
white crest unbridled by winter rains,
curdle and slip-slap, hurtle and skid
down a hail of rocks that clatter and
echo my clamoring chant.

Come, come, bustles the burbling brook
churning under winter's smitten branches,
green-fresh burstings hover, lilting wings
stream in the sun's drowsy beams, catkins
sloop festooned with yellow pollen caterpillars.
My surging shadow seeps into the shadows
of winged willows' sauntering dance, throat-
opening buds, excited yelps, humming
wheels speeding.

Spread-eagled on the road, purplish copper
wings close—unfold—squeeze shut—spring
open. Esme straddling her wooden two-wheeler
spies the note-plucker, looks and laughs, "You
have funny eyebrows!" "Yes, they got funnier
as I grew older." "Bye," she warbles, "bye,
Englishman,"and paddles along with her feet
beneath buckeye, willow, bay and oak. Contagion
bubbles. Shadow light ripples.

Where am I reeling, where am I whirling?
My gurgling vigor jingle-dingles: Down
the downy, down by the down, I follow
the hawk's lone cries to rootlets, adumbral
young ferns unfurling, the wood rat's elaborate

branched den, ant, weevil, worm, thread my way
past mossy logs, woodpeckers' nests, rampant
ivy, cow parsnip, leaping brambles, dark green
radiant thistles.

I gush along my banks with a skipping song,
while forget-me-nots tuck themselves in
ditches, dock and plantain spawn in rills,
shrills rise on penny royal's sharp aroma ,
hazel wands' leaves thrust from hidden
eyes, coral bells awkwardly slip out,
shadows flail across puddles, graceful
vultures circle, my simmering sap swirls
its way through your sap.

Perfume

This spirit breath
    leaves and enters
quite unbidden

Traveling light
    it bears
only essence

Let this perfume
    soak in your warmth
and pleasantness

each day and night
    of our
microscopic life

Earth

Each square inch
  a harmony
    of the dying
    the dead
  the living
and the being born

Composition For Choir by John Maas
and
Songs by Raphael Block

Strings of Shining Silence

poem (in its entirety on page 6) by Raphael Block; music by John Maas

for permission, contact John.M.Maas@gmail.com

Quarter note is about 60 bpm.

* "ting" is quiet and resonant but percussive like raindrops on metal; short vowel, straight to the "ng".

Blazing Trees, by Raphael Block

John Maas 2012

Rippling & Astir, by Raphael Block

No royalties for J Maas but please contact john.m.maas@gmail.com

John Maas

Songster, by Raphael Block

No royalties to J Maas but please contact John.M.Maas@gmail.com

John Maas

By the Shores of the Sea

Chorus

By the shores of the sea
waves pounding in glee
your sounds showed
me how to dance

A jig reeling inside
you made me step to your time
didn't care how I looked
to passersby

Playing to a hidden song
your crashing waves brought along

Chorus

Whirling round, round and round
lifted up and then plunged down

Playing to a hidden song
your crashing waves brought along

Chorus

Reaching out and reaching in
your silent songs set me in spin

Whirling round, round and round
lifted up and then plunged down

Playing to a hidden song
your crashing waves brought along

Chorus

Soak Up

Soak up my harmful thoughts,
wash them clean in morning mist
as redwood needles turn fog
into bountiful streams.

The apple trees lean, but
my thoughts lean even further—
I'm swayed by currents and
waves of feeling wronged.

Vultures perch on limbs
until this fog rises
and my heart is beside them
shivering in the cold.

How can I find the sun inside
so when the mist spirals away
and vultures dry their great wings
I, too, will lift up into day?

Soak up my harmful thoughts,
weave them into the fleeing mist
so my wings might stretch and soar
into this abundant day.

About the Author

Raphael's Block's poetry, infused with spirit, speaks to earth's call for a heartfelt response to our ecological crisis. Born on a kibbutz, he spent his boyhood playing on the hills of Haifa. His family returned to London as he turned nine, where learning British English shaped his ear for sound. In 1993 he moved to Northern California with his American wife, Deborah Simon Block, and their daughter, Theadora. His wife died from cancer in 2002, and over the following years it was his privilege to raise their child.

Raphael worked with children of all ages for almost 30 years. Since 2008, a life-threatening illness, Crohn's, has played a major role in intensifying his appreciation and gratitude for the moments of each day.

CPSIA information can be obtained
at www.ICGtesting.com
Printed in the USA
FSOW02n1542221016
26449FS